Dedication

Licensing for production and marketing

MEPASA AG
Winkelbüel 4
CH-6043 Adligenswil
Telephone   041 372 02 00
Telefax   041 372 02 01
www.mepasa.ch

Copyright
C by **IP** Institut für Persönlichkeitsentfaltung **AG**
Winkelbüel 4   CH-6043 Adligenswil
Telephone   041 372 06 66
Telefax   041 372 06 65
ip-ag@tic.ch
www.ipe.ch

Author   Franz X. Bühler

Translation   Heike Rudl

Illustrations   Pierre Bühler

Limited special edition german (Gold-Silver)   2002   out of print
Second edition german   2002
Third edition german   2004
fourth edition german   2005

English edition   ISBN 3-906439-16-X   2005

a rose for?

There are many participants needed for a book to be written, directly and indirectly. With these lines I also want to say thank you. Thank you to Tilli, my lovely wife, who had to spend many days and nights without me during the time of writing. Often I did not sleep because I was so excited and restlessly tossed in my bed from one side to the other. She read the book with the eyes of a reader and helped to improve with interesting and valuable ideas.

I also want to thank Heidy Gasser who stood at my side as an experienced author and lector; Barbara Wallimann, who with her extensive orthographical knowledge helped to create a book as professionally and correct as possible also for critical readers; my mother Emilie Bühler who swallowed up the emerging book with the eyes of a proof-reader and mother; Dr. Markus Wiggli who stole the time to round off the book with his knowledge and skill. And last but not least, Pierre Bühler (not related) who gave the book the final touch with his sensitive illustrations. Thank you very much!

to the author Franz X. Bühler
Born 1956 in Sursee (Switzerland). In a very personal process he has had many experiences and does not only teach on a theoretical basis but from practical experience, life. One of his outstanding abilities is to convey complex things easily and understandably. For more than 27 years the active study of life has been one of his great and fascinating tasks. Via various areas of education like mental training, suggestopedia and intensive studies of the sub-conscience, as trainer for NLP he came into contact with quantum physics and quantum psychology. He found the knowledge which fascinated him and which fulfils his demand for clarity and effectiveness. For Franz X. Bühler every human being is unique and precious. His approach towards him is characterised by esteem and respect.

He sees himself as a „learning teacher" and not as a master or guru. He is convinced of the wisdom of the individual and sees his task in awakening "the sleeping abilities" in everybody, in order to stay awake himself. Franz X. Bühler became known through his countless individual coachings, in which he helped many people to easily and quickly solve everyday problems, even of deep-seated nature, his learning strategy trainings, the ipower book-seminar, the IP-mind-method, fire walking seminars, the course „become slim-stay slim", the IP-Master training and the first comprehensive sideline mental and personality trainer school after VSMPT.

Preface

"The belly is the teacher of art"
(Persius Flaccus, Roman satirist, 34-62 ad.)

24 hours a day we live life. With eyes, ears, nose and mouth we grasp and understand our surroundings. Some of these experiences are gathered in our head, others find the way to our heart.

And we recognise: Many things are based on opposites. The one who is successful knows that he has to reorientate himself and to learn new things every day. That can be exciting and challenging. Every situation creates a new chance, assuming we are able and willing to see it.

What was valid yesterday will be redefined today. And this frequently without our personal involvement.

This fact pushes and encourages our mind and our preparedness to experience and create the future as open-minded human beings.

Among others, our experiences and insights are the basis for a mature way to go through life. Only with the knowledge that we have recognised with our mind and experienced with our heart, we act more instinctively than we are aware of.

This is good and makes us more secure in our actions and activities.

In the book „Out of the Head and into the Heart" you will read about experiences, insights and successes of fellow human beings – many times also little pieces of wisdom – which you can use personally and for your approach towards life.
In order for you to more frequently see the possibility, to live your life differently, maybe even more instinctively in a new way and with more success.

This dear reader is my wish for you, coming from my „belly" – excuse me – „from the bottom of my heart".

Peter Suter, Frick

this is what you will find in this book

I.
approaches to take you further

II.
**the largest department store for Projects, Goals
Wishes and Dreams**

9

10

V.
your thoughts – your goldmine

VI.
wealth – more than a word, within reach and feasible

VII.
wisdoms of great thinkers,
understand and convert to action

VIII.
habits that will be of help to you

IX.
things that make life easier

„how you can

read this book"

Who does Bühler think he is? As if I did not know how to read a very ordinary book. *»Very ordinary book? Excuse me, forget about it!«*

If you still have the feeling you could gain a new, fascinating idea, then you may curiously continue reading. You never know?

Well, one variation is:
Devour it from the beginning until the end. Take up the effective ideas, experiences, tips, yes even insights, which are thousands of years old. Let them sink in deep and critically observe their effectiveness and suitability in everyday life. Or just read it from the

beginning until the end, just like you mostly do it with other books.

The second possibility:
Whenever you are looking for a daily motto, just open up a page, because:
»Surprisingly often even coincidences can be of help.«

The third form:
Read only one chapter every day, be open and curious as to what you will discover and look forward to the next day full of expectations – just as if you had played the lottery and excitedly and nervously await your certain lotto jackpot.
After the first few months have passed, you can read it a second and a third time. I bet you, you will discover things which were hidden before. Who knows?

The fourth version…
…is the bibliomantical one. It almost has something magical and is only intended for persons who are willing to experiment. Despite that, are you interested? This is how it works:
»Close your eyes and ask a precise question, for which you are searching an answer for. Always keep this question in your head, while you now, still with closed eyes, take the book and start leafing through it full of expectations. Just open it up anywhere, point with your finger towards a spot and then open up your eyes. Which part did you find? To which part does your finger point?«

17

It may well be, that this special part in the book, provides you with valuable indications how you can progress in a matter. Sometimes it is the whole paragraph, often the whole page.

Be open, curious, willing to experiment and allow yourself to be surprised. Exceptional ideas can mean an effervescent source, a turbocharger in the development of a person. The one who believes to know everything and that there is nothing new to discover, will remain imprisoned in his limiting views. He simply remains still.

Remember: *»How many things were discovered and created by human beings during the last years alone? Things became possible which seemed unthinkable just 100 years ago? Things that you and I accept as an absolute matter of course and partly use everyday, like radio, television, broadcasting and computer, the train and many more things!«*

*Man nennt ihn Rohstein, den Diamanten,
der frisch aus dem Schoss der Erde ge-
hoben wurde. Klar in seiner Form, trübe
in der Ansicht. Verborgen sein Charakter.*

*Entdecke den
Diamanten in
Dir*

*It is called a rough stone, the diamond which was raised up
from the lap of the earth. Clear in its form, cloudy in its view.
Hidden its character. Discover the diamond within you.*

*They are within every human being and are often difficult to
discover – the diamonds which are only waiting to be
discovered and „cut"...*

„winners and losers

the difference?“

<unknown>

The looser is always a part of the problem.
The winner is always a part of the answer.
The looser always has an excuse.
The winner always has a programme.
The looser says: *»This is not my job.«*
The winner says: *»Let me do it for you.«*
The winner sees an answer in every problem.
The looser sees a problem in every answer.
The looser sees a problem in every sand hole.
The winner sees the green next to every sand hole.
The looser says: *»It could be possible but it is too difficult.«*
The winner says: *»It could be difficult but it is possible.«*
Which answers are yours?

„*there are no coincidences*"

<insight>

Attention: Today could be one of the most exciting and interesting days of your life. That's why you should make a decision: *»Is there such a thing as coincidence or not?«* You do not need to answer this immediately with YES or NO. Maybe this following insight will be of help to you:Thanks to intensive research in the area of quantum physics, scientists can prove today: *»There is no such thing as coincidence. But incidents happen, the connection of which we cannot consciously re-enact with a cause, when they happen!«* That is amazing! If there are definitely no coincidences, you could conclude from your adventures and experiences, that there are certain contents saved somewhere in your life and therefore your super computer which is called brain. These attract things, which you sometimes do not like, which you may have wanted to be different. Start now and closely look at the „coincidences" in your life. I also needed more than 50 „coincidences" before I, being a rational electrical engineer had to admit reluctantly: *»There are no coincidences!«* Question: *»What happened to you coincidentally during the past few weeks and months?«*

„the story of the eagle"

<unknown>

There once was a wonderful, speckled eagle egg, that fell into a strange, soft nest. Despite the fact, that it looked completely different than the others, the hens decided, after discussing back and forth, to sit on it. Time went by and a strange chick hatched. Months passed, the chicks grew and learned, what a „real chicken" is. One day the little eagle saw a large majestic bird flying up in the air. *»Oh if I could only fly like that«* was his greatest wish. The chicken clucked excitedly: *»that is nothing for „the likes of us". That is much too dangerous, we cannot fly that high!«*
If the little eagle will ever learn to fly so majestically soley depends on his belief to be „the likes of us" or if he just tries and spreads his majestic wings.
What are the beautiful and great things of which you believe that they are nothing for you – nothing for „the likes of us"? When will you just start to tackle them and act?

„even the longest way starts

with the first step"

<unknown>

When I had the idea for this book, I thought: *»When will you be able to pack this in your busy calendar?«* But then I had a fascinating thought: *»If I only write one page a day, I will be finished at the latest in 168 days!«* The thought shot up my pulse and a warm, unusually powerful and encouraging feeling started to spread within my stomach. In the end, I often wrote several pages a day and the book was finished sooner that planned!

No matter what plans you have, how huge „your" mountains in front of you seem to be: *»Think, plan and then progress step by step. Progress full of confidence and motivation towards your goal!«*

And always remember: *»A mile consists of a 1000 steps, a fortune worth a million consists of a million pounds. Every step, every pound is needed to reach the goal you strived for.«*

„Love –

something for dreamers?"

<Love as a tool for realists and other "crackpots">

Love is supposedly the biggest power we know? What is meant by that? Everything is fine, everything is in order, everything pink? No! To love something means to like it with all its facets, to accept it, not to quarrel with it, not to doubt it.

To love means: »*Direct your whole energy towards the thing you really desire from the bottom of your heart. Be moved, even excited about it with every fibre, every molecule, every atom of your body. Swing, vibrate and shake because of excitement, when you think of your idea! Become the idea yourself – be your idea!*«

Successful people ask themselves:

»*What do I love about…..? What can I do to ….. love even more and more intensive? What makes ….. especially loveable? What strengthens my belief, that ….. is really possible?*«

25

„*I am precious*"

<desirable basic feeling as suggestion>

The quantum physicist Ulrich Warnke plausibly pre-calculated that the energy value of only 1 gramme of human material, when recalculated, has a monetary value of an unbelievable 1 million dollars!

Which fairly reasonable human being cannot – only on a materialistic basis – say about himself he is not precious? Sure you need more than that. To feel that you are a precious person and to be convinced of your inner and outer values, you must develop a strong and deep feeling for who you really are!

The following exercise worked like a miracle for many: »*Ask yourself what makes you valuable to other people? Is it your experience, your knowledge, your reliability, your sensitivity, your abilities? What do you really appreciate about yourself? What valuable experiences have you made, that helped others (and you)?*« Write everything on a piece of paper and read it for 60 days – every day – at least 3 times, once before you sleep!

You are not only what can be touched, you are everything that is inside your head. This makes you unique and precious!

„*tolerating details*

will be the beginning of the end"

<Ralph Krueger, coach of the Swiss National Hockey Team>

Rigorous discipline is one of the main keys to your success. When you start being slack and compliant even with little things, first, small, mean success preventers inevitably start to build a nest in your subconscience! A small, inconspicuous tyrant, who brilliantly knows how to sabotage your motivation a little more every day until it is completely destroyed, wilted into a small pile of misery, lying on the floor.

This is why you should set small, achievable interim goals, because you will be able to handle and grab these more consequently.

Only take one step a day. Work with discipline and never stop before you have achieved them!

Test yourself:

»What are the feelings that you have when you look back and see that you consequently realised what you had planned? Are you not a little proud? And what influence does that have on your self-confidence?«

„believe in the impossible and the impossible becomes possible"

<Ralph Krueger>

In the understanding of our language the word "impossible" is absolute and does not leave a way out. Really? Is it not exactly the other way round? "Impossible" also contains the word "possible"!. And the syllable "im" also almost stands for "not like that"! So it does not mean "impossible", but "not like that possible". But this is the pure opposite. It means: "There is always a way. You just have not found it yet."

Maybe you are just missing the strong conviction, that you can really do it? Then ask yourself:*<What can you do today to strengthen your conviction towards the 100% success? Mentally? Actively through actions?>*

Is it not marvellous to know that other people, even before you, were in that same or a similar tricky situation and that they succeeded? <Everything that a person ever succeeded in, you can also achieve. Because you work with the same recipes and laws, as everybody else!>

28

„*you have a problem?*

Good – you are alive!"

<Napoleon Hill>

Why is it that so many people have difficulties with the word problem? Is it really your wish not to have any problems or challenges? I only know one location where all the people do not have any problems: the graveyard!
Problems that we mastered, make us strong, experienced and more precious in many respects.
Bear in mind: »*you can not have a problem – or call it challenge – without the core of the solution already being in you.*« That is pure polarity. The knowledge of this fact can give you confidence to approach it rather than to avoid it or being crushed by it. Believe me: »*To avoid a problem does not bring you any further, I tried it too many times, it never worked! The challenge was thrown back at me again and again only in different clothing – but at its core it remained the same.*« Tackle the problem in its depth, think about the actions that brought you there. Recognise it and change! You will be surprised…

„Failures?“

For most people failures are incidents that completely demotivate them, they sap their energy and they are set back in their goals. Even worse, they are able to let their dreams burst like soap bubbles! That cannot and should not be!

Failure only really becomes a failure if you evaluate the result. Never evaluate! Failures are also results just like success. Learn from them and avoid producing the same result a second time!

Your whole life consists of «go, no-go» results. Even when you learned to walk, this was the case. Did you give in after the 100th time and did you say: *»I will never learn this?«* Hardly, otherwise you would still be scraping your knees and creeping and crawling! You tried it a 101st time and a 102nd time until it worked.

The following approach will help you to draw power from "failures": *»View every result as a neutral result, an impressive and valuable investment in your learning and growing. Accept it thankfully because it will take you further.«*

The most popular people are people with experience. But experiences are not something you learned rather experiences that you learned from!

„a ship is safe in the harbour,

but that is not what it was built for"

<unknown>

Are you one of the people who prefer to stay in the safe harbour, than daring themself into the open waves of life? Well, then it is high time to leave the harbour. Discover the world and life, it can be marvellous! There is a much better navigator within you than you think. Prepare your journey, become fit and take action. You will see, the handling of the rudder and the sails is easier than you think, and what you are not able to do, you will be taught by the journey.

Enjoy the whipping white caps, the wind that blows in your face and that takes your breath away, enjoy the challenges. They are the special something, the spicy flavour, they are a part of life. Yes they are even more than that: *»They are your real friend, without them you will not proceed, they will take you to new shores of life and accompany you.«* Set your sails and begin!

„only the one who strives for the impossible, is successful in achieving the possible"

<unknown>

Nice words, but what if I set my goal too high and don't achieve it? Stress and frustration are pre-programmed. Are they not?

No! They are not if you only consider one condition: *»Always enjoy what you have achieved so far, even if it does not correspond to your huge goal – and go on striving for the impossible.«*

Great goals activate great ideas, small goals open small drawers. Test it yourself. What ideas do you have when asking yourself: *<What do I have to do to earn 10% more in one year?>* And what happens when the question reads as follows: *»What do I have to do to double my earnings of what I now make in one year?«*

Bear in mind: *»Everything that has been achieved by somebody before you, can also be achieved by you! You have the same possibilities, you live on the same earth and you follow the same universal laws.«*

„be thankful"

<unknown>

Be thankful for everything you have, your health, your knowledge, your expertise, your environment, your wealth, your job, your neighbour, your life. If you have a wish, then ask the universal intelligence, God, Jesus, or whatever you may call it, for it to become true. And now the most important thing: *»Be thankful that it already became true in your thoughts, that it is the case!«*

To many people this may sound pretty hard to get used to and also sanctimonious. But it is not. In quantum physics it is even the absolute hit tip!

Why?

Because the „being thankful for something" – especially in the form, in which „already became true" means nothing else than anchoring the complete picture of success.

And the best of it: *»Being thankful for something which has been achieved is one of the most perfect forms of letting go«*

- according to quantum physics comprehensible!

„*a smile is the nicest way*

to show others

your teeth"

<unknown>

Or as Arthur Lassen once described it: »*The smile is the shortest connection between two people.*« Smile more than others! A lot can be done easier with a smile on your face. Even if you don't feel like smiling today: »*Smile and feel the wonderful effect, it is like soothing your troubled soul.*«
It has been found out that smiling uses 50% less of your muscles than when you frown.
Make a decision: »*Do you want to feel bad and still have the bigger „cramp" or do you want to feel powerful, motivated and good?*« Make the following test: »*Smile as often as possible. Smile at other people and observe what comes back!*« Mostly you will be given a nice smile in return. And if somebody can't deal with that, it's his problem not yours.

„*I love dealing with people,*

people love dealing with me"

<Hans Peter Zimmerman>

Does your job include dealing with people? Do you have a leading position? Is selling your profession? Then make this test. It is astonishing how these few words, if they are embodied deep down within, change a whole life!

When I daily read this sentence out loud for months more than 300 times a day and almost bit my tongue doing that, wondrous things started to happen. I was in a better mood, people approached me more openly, I was welcomed and was given appointments with astonishing easiness, I doubled my sales quota – and today I have one of the nicest and most exciting jobs in the world: »*I am allowed to help people develop.*« Just because of this sentence? Who knows? »*What you exude, comes back to you!*« Make your own decision.

„*I can do it…I will do it…*

I am great"

<*auto-suggestive credos*>

Have you ever asked yourself, what it is about the Japanese celebrating with shouting and jumping every morning or what is going on among rugby sides when they build a „pile" and shout out their battle cries? They get into the mood and psyche themselves up!

And can you give me one good reason why this shouldn't work for you?

The loser's answer will be: »*Yes, but I can't do it, what would the others say…?*« The winner's answer will be: »*Why not…!*«

Test it yourself and only then make a decision…

The exercise is done like this: »*Take a deep breath, smile and then with lifted arms say out loud „yeeees, I can do it, I am able to do it, I am greeaat!"*« and do this again for 10 times… And if you want to increase the effectiveness, do it with the (your) whole team. »*We are what?…Greeeaaat!*«

36

„*change from the*

« *Yes-Butter> to a <Why-Notter»!*"

<Klaus Kobjoll>

Long before they are really disclosed and they express their basic approach towards life, you can already recognise them through their words! The winner type says: »*Why not…*« and in their answer the chance of finding a feasible way is swinging along. They are looking for solutions!

The looser will say: »*Yes, but…*« and their „but" has often the effect of a hammer blow. Note: apologies, excuses and objections (almost) always start with a „but".

Make a decision now: »*Do you want to change something in your life, find a new way, achieve goals, let wishes and dreams come true? Or do you want to prove that this does not work just with you?*

Do you want to be successful or right?«

Change from a „Yes-Butter" to a „Why-Notter", for the sake of your wishes and your dreams!

Er ist der vornehmste aller Steine. Er
kann nur mit seinem eigenen Pulver ge-
ritzt werden, in keiner Hitze geschmolzen
noch durch eine Flüssigkeit gelöst.
werden. Nur das heftigste künstliche
Feuer verwandelt ihn endlich voll-
ständig in farblose Luft welche die-
selbe ist, die der Most beim Übergange
zum Wein entwickelt. Kohlenstoff

*It is the most distinguished stone of them all. It can only be
scratched with its own powder, not melted in any heat, nor
dissolved by any fluid.*
*Only the most fierce artificial fire finally changes it into
completely colourless air, which is the same carbon that
develops when juice converts into wine.*

*Finally they are laying before you – the raw diamonds,
discovered, cut, ready to be awakened by skilful hands. What
„precious" winner might be hidden behind the rough surface?*

„Losers say:

I will try"

<unknown>

You do not have to try it, you just simply do it! The word „trying" subliminally includes the open backdoor: »I tried, it did not work« – to then surrender.

What did not work? Nothing failed! The outcome was simply not as you expected or which you just didn't want.

Or did you even say: »That is what I was afraid of?« Well, great that means, you have stirred up an expectation that you didn't want!

You do not to have be afraid of anything, if you accept results simply as what they are: »results!«

Winner types say: »I will do it!« and if they don't like the result, they will do it again, this time differently because they have learned how it doesn't work. So from today on, what is your Motto that takes you further? »Yes, I will do it!«

„no time to attend seminars,

read books,

do further training?"

<unknown>

Read the following story:

»A wanderer meets a woodcutter, who is trying to chop down a tree. His saw is totally blunt and he hardly progresses. *„Sharpen your saw blade, then you will be able to saw better and will be much faster"* says the wanderer. The woodcutter replies: *„I don't have time to do that – I have to saw…"«* When, how and with what do you sharpen your „saw blade"? When do you take the time to do further training? Plan it, and now take the first step – you know, within 72 hours. It could be a phone call with which you make inquiries and get important information and notes, an exciting book that you order, an unconventional magazine that you buy, an honest complement that you consciously make.

When, how and with what do you sharpen your „saw blade"?

40

„*the freedom to be a crackpot*"

<unknown>

Every day we much too often strive to fulfil other peoples' various expectations, full of concentration act as „it" should be? But would we sometimes not rather flip out, just like that – without any reason – flip out a little and break rigid rules…
Many times we hesitate by asking the question that destroys everything: *»What will the others say?«* You know what: *»Firstly many people would like to do the same – and secondly it is completely irrelevant what others say or think.«* That is their problem. You are allowed to flip out! Yes I ask you: *»Every now and then just flip out!«* People will learn to accept it. After a while you will even get the „stamp" to be a crackpot. That is the best that can happen to you!. Now you can live your newly achieved freedom, whenever you want, like the motto:*»It is not a surprise that a crackpot like him does something like that.«* I, on my part, enjoy the freedom to be a crackpot. The only thing that you should pay attention to: *»Be careful that you do not harm anybody.«* (sowing and harvesting!)

„*only ask for advice,*

if you are ready to accept it"

<Franz X. Bühler>

Many people ask others for advice. But they are basically just seeking for confirmation that they did something right or even that they know better. That is just like pouring wine into a glass that is already full and even running over. Just forget it! It can't hold anymore.

So before you ask somebody for advice, ask yourself: *»Am I honestly open for and interested in this piece of advice, am I prepared to accept it and to change something?«*

Empty your glass with preconceived ideas and prepare it for new contents.

Great is not the one who thinks to be able to do everything himself. Great is the one who knows that he has „weaknesses" just like everybody else and who is prepared to learn. And even greater is the one, who knows that even in his strongest point he can learn from others and is honestly prepared to do it.

„what is more important,

to know a lot or to understand it

and live it?"

Are you one of the many impatient people who are searching and collecting? The people who full of hope devour a book, absorb one seminar after the other, finish degree after degree, constantly seek advice, always hoping to loosen their big button. I bet you that you know the answer already – within yourself! I know many people who have an impressively large and broad knowledge. Sadly they have it only in their head and not in their heart. And when they have finally understood it, they are just one step further, then the motto is: *»live!«* To know how something works does not help at all. You have to build it into your fascinating life, it must become a part of you and daily shape your life. The following questions may be of help to you. *»What does this knowledge mean for me? How and where can it affect my life? What is the deeper meaning behind it?«*

II.

the largest department store for projects, goals, wishes and dreams

„dream your life,

live your dream"

<unknown>

But in order to live your dream life you must first dream it, that is why it is called "dream life"! When did you dream the last time? Not during the night, no I mean "day dreaming" and having your head in the clouds, think of your world in pink and sky-blue?
You should dream more often. More powerful resources are hidden behind that, than you would think. Play some relaxing music tonight, sit down and make yourself comfortable. Close your eyes and imagine what you would do if money wasn't important, your existence would be completely secured and you could live off the interest. Your long strived for around the world vacation lies behind you and all you want is to have fun and joy from what you do all day long. What would you do?

„the largest department store?

The Universe!"

<Bärbel Moor>

There is only one "department store" in which you can order everything that you wish: »*The Universe!*« You can order everything that your heart is striving for and if you do everything right, it will even be delivered. But there is one thing you must pay attention to: »*The order must be clear and straightforward, otherwise it will be difficult for the hard-working creatures in the shipping company to deliver the right thing to you.*« They are not interested in what you want, they only want to know what your wishes are!

»*But that is obvious*« do you think? Then listen to people when they „order". Most of them only talk about what they don't want. They don't want debts, no disobedient children, not such a lousy job, not a mean husband, no unreliable secretary, no customers with bad credit. This means they precisely order what they don't want. If you know exactly what you want, write it down and „send" it away. But put enough stamps on it, so that it really will be delivered. Stamps? Load it up with feelings like joy and enthusiasm!

„*ordering in the Universe...*

lesson 2"

<Franz X. Bühler>

Of course you can place your order several times, just to be on the safe side. It wouldn't be necessary, if you "stuck" enough postage on your letter! Constantly ordering the same thing every day is the same as if you carried your order with you all the time, but would never send it away!

Letting go is the magic word.

Let us summarise:

1. Your order has to be put in the right words.
2. You need enough postage.
    (power, joy, enthusiasm, motivation)
3. Imagine what it would be like to accept the delivery yourself.
4. Let go, forget the order, now you are busy building the delivery ramp. (keep your eyes on the goal, work hard, keep your eyes on the responses and programmes)

„wishing alone

is not enough"

<Franz X. Bühler>

The desire to change something must be deep inside yourself. The drive comes, as always, from your sub-conciousness. The wish won't be enough to make your sub-conciousnessplay a different melody! First, you have to put in a different CD and start to think and act like that!
It is not enough if you want to be rich. You have to change your ways in order to become rich. It is not enough if you want to be smart and educated. You have to start to continue your studies, to read and attend further training courses. It is not enough if you want to be a loving person. You have to start to think lovingly, to love yourself and to discover what it is in others that is worth loving.
Your wish is the seed.
It is you who has to nurture and grow it!

„the quality of your goals

determines the quality

of your future"

Do you have small goals which are hardly worth mentioning? Or are you disillusioned and powerless by all these dead sure success strategies because they only seem to work for others? That is a pity, because I can assure you that you are missing some of the most wonderful and exciting things in life: »*The setting and achieving of personal goals and the indescribable magnificent feelings that come with it.*«
Do you remember when you started to learn how to walk, when you took your first cautious and clumsy steps which became larger and more and more confident every day?
It is the same with goals. Start small. Start thinking into which dream direction shall they take you – and then practice, practice and practice! Goals are response patterns, which you save in your sub-conscience. If you have small goals, small things will happen. If you have great goals, great things can happen. It is as simple as that! But you have to „do" it!

„projects, goals?

first why,

then how and what with?"

You want to tackle something and realise it, you have projects, wishes, dreams and goals? Good!

Then firstly ask yourself: *»Why? Why do you want to succeed? What do you gain? What kind of feeling arises when you imagine that you have already succeeded?«*

The question for the „why" shows you how strong your motivation today already is to achieve this goal. It is the irreplaceable power which you will need along your exciting way. Sometimes you hit stumbling blocks and other hurdles. Then you will need the power of motivation in order to keep on walking into the direction of your goal.

Motivation has one of its roots in the answers to the „why"! Only when you definitely and clearly know why this goal is so important to you, ask yourself: *»How and with what will I definitely achieve this goal?«*

„are you also

Mr. or Ms. 95%?"

«Franz X. Bühler»

When I was still working in the sales of highly complex, electronic measuring instruments, something very special happened. No matter how high my boss set the budget: *»I always achieved 95%!«* This made me think. Today I know that it was my self-confidence and my self-assurance which led me to performances which were always short of the goal. I didn't feel good enough to achieve 100%. Not me …!?

Since I have realised this, I always set my goals in the way that 95% are still at least 20% higher than the result of last year and I thoroughly plan in order to really achieve it. By this I constantly increase my performance. And what is very important: *»I learned to be happy about 95% because they are also precious – and I am too!«* Sometimes you just have to know how to trick your „programmes" and then everything is much easier.

„the wheel of fortune,

your goal programmer"

<derived from a Tibetan prayer wheel by Franz X. Bühler>

You have a goal, a wish, a dream? Good. Now write everything down what you now have at your disposal in order to achieve it and what can actively contribute: *»abilities, environment, knowledge, characteristics, money, partner, people, books, attended seminars and trainings, institutions, and so on.«*
Then you draw yourself a wheel with a large hub in the middle. Write your goal into the hub. The spokes will be the characteristics and abilities listed above and so on. Colour it really cheeky and mod. The more varied and loud, the better! Then you stick it on a piece of cardboard, cut it and mount a small wave in its middle. Now you stick it into something where it can be turned effortlessly. Make yourself comfortable, watch your bubbly wheel and glide with it into the miraculous world of your wishes. If you now play or sing your favourite music, it will even reach deeper and more intensively into your sub-conscience, your goal programmer!

III.

Tools for success, light, easy and effective

„success is what follows,

when you follow yourself"

<Klaus Kobjoll>

Do you know the story of the young cat, that is chasing its tail and was always running in circles? One day an older cat came along and asked: *»What are you doing?«* The young one replied: *»You know I went to cat philosophy school and we learned that luck and success is at home in our tails. So if I chase my tail long enough, some day I will grab my luck.«* The older cat said. *»That is interesting. I never went to such a school but I have noticed that my luck follows me when I walk in the direction of my dreams!«*
And the moral of this story:
»You don't need to chase your luck and success. Just do what you are able to do, what you dream about, follow your gut feelings, walk full of confidence in the direction of your wishes, dreams and goals and your luck and success will follow you!«

„the recipe

for results"

<Franz X. Bühler>

-   deactivate your distracting responses...
    (relax, close your ordinary weekday drawers…)
-   activate your power
    (lift your spirit, your energy…)
-   activate your goal responses…
    (put your goal pictures into your memory…)
-   fully concentrate…
    (only do what is now important to you, that will take you further…)
-   every 60 minutes switch on a 10-minute "letting go phase"
    (get up, do something different, have a cup of tea, coffee or a glass of water)

Oeffne sein Herz

Wie der Urknall trifft ein klarer, bestimmter Schlag den Diamanten, damit er sich öffnen kann um die Schönheit seines Herzens Preis zugeben die sich erst erahnen lässt. Die Erkenntnis seiner selbst erfolgt durch das Herz.

Like the Big Bang a clear distinct blow hits the diamond in order for it to open and to be able to reveal the beauty of its heart, which before can only be suspected. The discovery of itself takes place through the heart.

Now it goes stride by stride – step by step – according to an exactly laid out, well-tried plan into the direction successful revelation of the valuable treasure.

„the 7 steps to success"

<Franz X. Bühler>

Who does not search for the effective recipe, which can be used for every project in life, starting with love, partnership, business and money? Now you have found it!

I guarantee you: »*If you follow it step by step, you will find great success, which yesterday seemed unreachable to you.*«

But I warn you:

»*Just by reading and knowing, nothing will happen – it is you who has to "cook" it!*«

And this is how it works…

1. Is-analysis	…where do you stand?
2. Goals	…what is your direction?
3. Planning	…how do you get there?
4. Training	…what do you need for that?
5. Working	…from knowing to DOING!
6. Control	…where am I on the way?
7. Letting go	…switch off success preventers!

"the 7 steps to success

today: the Is-analysis"

Question: How do you want to plan your sailing trip if you at this point in time do not know in which harbour your ship anchors? How do you want to establish your course for success if you do not exactly know where you stand? Forget it, you don't have a chance! Every step could take you closer to, or further from your goal. You simply don't know!

The key question is: »*Where exactly do you stand? Financially? In regards to family affairs? In regards to your job? Abilities? Do you regularly eliminate your mental blocks? Do you regularly set daily goals, which lead towards your inspiring goals? Do you like to work? Can you let go? Are you often angry, full of envy? Are you concerned? Are you often afraid of the future? Are you honest, persevering, disciplined, full of joie de vivre and enthusiasm? Do you think positive and goal-oriented? Do you like to make decisions and do you like to make them fast? Do you always sleep enough? Are you able to concentrate? Do you trust yourself and others? Are you an organisational talent, kind, balanced, healthy?*«

Extend above list of questions in regards to your goals!

"the 7 steps to success

today: my goal (s)"

Because you now know in which harbour your ship of life anchors, you can keep on sailing. Now your motto is: »*Where shall the journey lead? What is it exactly that you want? What would you like to achieve? What is your goal?*« In the chapter „SMART" you will learn more about how goals have to be put into words, so that you have the best chances!

And now immediately do something for your motivation. It is the fire that you constantly have to fan, so that underway you have the power to withstand even very strong storms! And then imagine what it would look like when you have achieved your goal. And very important: »*See yourself in this movie! Who takes part in your joy? How do you recognise that you have achieved your goal? How does it feel? What do you hear that others say to you?*« Even now feel the joy of having achieved your goal!

How great your goals should be? Very simple:
»*Set yourself great goals, then there is a lot of power!*«
Small ones we loose sight of when the first obstacles arise. Split your goal into many small stages. General rule: »*You should achieve intermediate goals within three days.*«

„the 7 steps to success

today: planning"

Now that you know in which harbour your yacht anchors, the wanderlust starts to grow within yourself and how well equipped your ship of life already is, the next duel is awaiting you: »*Your motivation against your lethargy!*«
Is all that necessary? Isn't there a simpler way?
Do you want to or don't you want to? You want to?
Ok, then now the planning has to start.
The following questions will help you: »*What is still necessary to achieve your goal? Material? Knowledge? Relationships? Abilities? Institutions? How and with what do you intend to get there? What could help you to faster achieve your wonderful goal? What activities will take you a step further towards your goals every day? What is when – and how important? (Priority list) Who needs to be contacted in that respect? What do you need to know to thoroughly make your plans? What intermediate goals would you like to achieve? What is your reward when you achieve your intermediate goals and your final goal?*« The best is to start a „journey file". On every page write down one of the questions mentioned above and then: »*Off you go and have lots of fun.*«

„the 7 steps to success

today: **training"**

If your goal is so great that today you still see it as an un-surmountable mountain, you most likely need a few abilities which need to be trained. You would hardly go on a Himalayan Tour without having succeeded training on the relevant, more simple routes. Or would you?

Therefore: *»What do you need to acquire, to know in order to achieve your goal and when on your way do you need these abilities?«*

What convictions do you need in order to stay disciplined and what suggestions will help you with that?

Is your list completed? Well, then off you go! Congratulations, you have managed another hurdle in order to sail your ship safely through violent storms into the acclaimed harbour of your goal.

Here you will find another idea so that your tough training brings even more joy every day in order to make the attraction irresistible, yes even magical for you: *»Build a goal collage with pictures which contain your inspiring goal. Write the relevant goal title on top and „draw" this picture in a few times every day!«*

„the 7 steps to success

today: **working"**

What comes now, has to be done. It has to be a part of it, like the path towards the goal; sometimes pretty troublesome, sometimes motivating, sometimes you take it humming a song, another time sluggishly, crawling, staggering or laboriously climbing.

Now you need to work, convert into action, breathe life into your vision and consequently go your way step by step!

As you already know, it is very helpful if you divide your journey into little steps. Steps which you can finish within three days or even earlier. Why? Because your motivation grows with every finished step. It is the fire that warms along the way, when it gets cold and it is your power station. Should your power threaten to vanish.

Another sound reason not to plan rigid time frames is: *»Rigid time frames slow you down, they restrict you and keep you from being able to let go. They dismantle your motivation in case you should not be within your „time frame". It is better to start without a time frame but totally motivated and full of power.«* Often you will achieve great goals within a third of the planned time!

„the 7 steps to success

today: controlling, rewarding"

Did you know that only about 3% of all people consider themselves successful? You have made it up to here. That proves: »*You have the tools to belong to that group.*« Welcome on your next step to success!

On this page you will get to know two tools. The first one is your most important navigation tool and the second – be surprised – is so to speak your psychological dynamite!

To the first…

Your intermediate tools, as is your final goal, have to be clearly controllable and measurable! The question which might help with this reads as follows: »*How do you recognise that you proceeded another step ahead; that you have fulfilled the next task on your path or even achieved your goal?*«

Check daily where you are on your journey.

The second – your dynamite…

Reward yourself for every larger successfully achieved step (think of the 3 daily tasks!) and lay down the rewards for that even today! With this your subconciousness works from reward to reward. Test it and you will be amazed!

„*the 7 steps to success*

today: **letting go**"

»*You simply have to let go…*« is one of the most mentioned clichéd pieces of advice.

»*As if I didn't know that myself! – How can I let go, if the debts worry me and the creditors remind me painfully of them everyday? How can I let go and become well again, when my illness shows me everyday that I am still weak and without energy? How can I let go of a goal, when I am proceeding towards it full of energy and when I am even supposed to measure it every day?*«

»*Let go of having to get there, in your thoughts already be at your goal! Make your order in the Universe and forget it – until the next time. Wanting to fight for something and trying to get it by force means becoming tense, trying to hold onto it.*«

You are also OK if you achieve your goal at just 90% – if it was great enough your are still very much ahead of everybody else!

It was just like that with this book. Every page was another step, a small success!

Further ideas to let go you will find on page 157.

„*checking goals*

according to SMART"

<Tad James>

Tad James' formula „SMART" is plain and ingeniously simple to check goals, wishes and dreams. Use some of you time right now. It is one of the most rewarding investments and will pay you back 10, yes even 100 times!

S = specific and clear *(how do you recognise that you have achieved your goal?)*

M = measurable *(how and by what do you recognise that you have come closer to your goal?)*

A = as if *(put your goal into words as if you had already achieved it)*

R = realistic *(your mind must believe that it is possible)*

T = timeless *(when possible always plan steps of success instead of time frames)*

„only what you measure

gets improved"

<Patrick T. Robson – CEO of a rental company for measuring instruments>

Only what you measure can really be improved. If you don't check regularly where you stand, you will not realise when you have strayed off the path. Sometimes a side effect that slows you down and prevents success is created: »Soon you will loose motivation, the inner fire that spurs you on, because you cannot see that you goal comes closer every day!«

On the whole, measuring is one of the most important factors for success. Every responsible pilot constantly checks the course. If he gets off the course due to cross winds, he will correct it. It doesn't come to any pilot's mind to stubbornly keep on flying and land at the planned time, no matter if there is a runway or not.

Bottom line: »Measuring offers you the possibility to recognise and if necessary correct – and it creates an invaluable, yes payless side effect: Power, motivation and a burning desire!«

„when things are

becoming too much"

<associated and dissociated – a finding from NLP>

Then the following exercise can help you effectively. Close your eyes and bring the oppressing problem on your screen, your inner movie screen. Now directly enter that burdensome movie and experience it in your thoughts with all its unpleasant details and facets – very real – once again. Then you clap your hands loud and hard and leave this movie momentarily like a flash. Change from being someone who experiences to someone who observes! Imagine you are a bird or a fly, which full of excitement observes you from 5-10 metres in this situation. It is very important that: *»You see yourself in this picture!«*

Now change the brightness, the light of this picture so that your feelings, when you are observing this picture, become more and more neutral and pleasant. That is very easy because now you are the director of your movies, of your life.

And now you ask yourself the following question: *»How can this person (you), who you are observing right now, solve his problem?«*

IV.

Insights,
true and suitable
for everyday life

„what positive thinking

really is"

<Franz X. Bühler>

Ask other people what they understand by „positive thinking" and the general tenor will always sound like whitewashing of experiences and putting on the pink glasses, like the motto: »*Look, the whole thing also has a positive side, you just have to think positively, then everything will be fine.*«
Wrong!
That is positive thinking in the sense of „evaluating". Short term it can give you a better feeling, but comes more to a convulsive suppression and it makes you ill. You will not solve a problem by suppressing it or by whitewashing it!
On the first look you seem to contradict the HUNA principle „*your world-is-what-you-think-of-it*". But you *don't*.
Real positive thinking is goal-oriented thinking! You think of something that you really want. In reference to a goal, wish or dream this means, you think with a „*that-is-the-way-I-would-like-to-have-it attitude*" and not what you want. How do you think? Think and it is.

„*your environment shapes*

your future"

<Franz X. Bühler>

Yes, even more than that , your environment offers great opportunities to become your future. Today you are what you are because of your genetic predisposition, your education, your experiences, school, the choice of media, your further education, books, television and radio, the culture in which you grew up and the environment in which you were raised. All of that had a deep impact on you and shaped who you are.

Don't you like your "Today"? You can only change it, if you choose new, other „Inputs" for your supercomputer, your brain.

Change your environment and your relations, choose different media and trainings. This will lead you to different experiences and different people. Do you want to belong to the winner group? Surround yourself with winners! That doesn't mean you should pack your tent and leave. Choose wisely, well-thought over and then follow this path, consequently with joy and perseverance.

„I looked back and saw that the stones along my way turned into the stairs to success"

<Franz X. Bühler>

Sure, as long as you are suffering under the pressure of a massive problem it will not be your cup of tea. But especially the wonderful insight mentioned above (*read it one more time and let it melt on your tongue*) can give you the additionally required kick right in moments like that, to finally take the bull by its horns and to tackle the challenge full of power. From every result, some call it mistake, we can learn. The one who makes mistakes is not foolish, the one who constantly makes the same mistake is foolish.

A wise man once said: *»Do you want to double your success, then double your mistakes!«*

So now look back kindly and wisely knowing and ask yourself: *»What resulted from your biggest mistake? What have you learned from it? What has changed positively due to that?«*

„*enthusiasm is one of the highest paid characteristics in the world*"

<Franz X. Bühler>

Life as a whole is one form of selling. If you bring up children, "sell" your partner an idea, make a raise appealing to your boss, recommend a product to a customer, it is always „selling".

From whom would you rather buy something, from a grumpy de-motivated, negatively talking salesperson or from somebody who is motivated, well-informed, beaming and enthusiastic?

Make up a (your) list of 30 things that you are enthusiastic about! Write them down, collect photos about everything that brings you joy and fun. The list should contain little things of everyday life as well as the great experiences. And then see, what you feel like after 20 minutes! Now be enthusiastic about yourself, life, your tasks, your partner and do everything that you do with enthusiasm. It will pay back a thousand times!

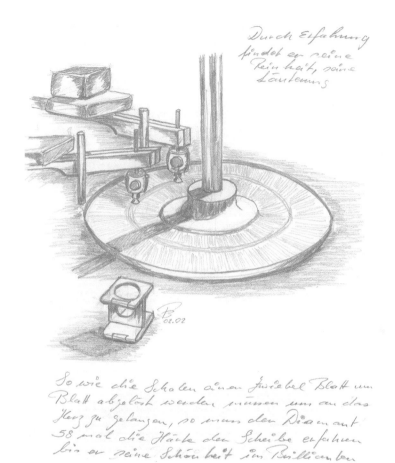

*Durch Erfahrung
findet er seine
Reinheit, seine
Läuterung*

*So wie die Schalen einer Zwiebel Blatt um
Blatt abgelöst werden müssen um an das
Herz zu gelangen, so muss der Diamant
58 mal die Härte der Scheibe erfahren
bis er seine Schönheit im Brillanten*

*Like the skins of an onion that have been peeled away layer
by layer, in order to get to the heart, the diamond has to
experience the hardness of the disc 58 times for it to show its
beauty as a cut diamond.
The diamond is now cut lovingly and enduringly with fine work,
in order to release its sparkling, valuable core a little more
every hour.*

„as above – so below,

as within – so without"

<Hermes>

You act as you think. Your world and your whole life is shaped the same way it looks inside you.
Are there things in your life, which you would like to have differently? Instead of caustic, corroding, indecisive and insidious, rather fascinating and exciting, driven by a desire shaking of excitement? Then you have to start thinking and acting differently today.
The true story: »*There was this person whose office looked the same as it did in his head – completely chaotic! He flipped from one idea, one thought to the next, was torn back and forth and never came to a proper result. Only when he started to clean up, did his situation change.*«

»*Clean up outside – and your „inside" will follow. Clean up inside – and your „outside" will follow. It doesn't matter where you start, clean up and it will be effective!*«

„nothing in the world is as powerful as an idea, the time of which has come"

<unknown>

Nobody can stop an idea, if the time for it has come. The only question is: *»When is that?«* Question: *»Why is that so important?«*

Did you ever have the feeling that you were ahead of the times with your ideas? And did you even loose money because you wanted to "land" people with something? Did you then give up and years later became annoyed about the fact that others became rich with "your" idea? That is a pity!

You only made one single mistake: *»You didn't use the lead and wanted to accomplish something by force!«* Especially because you were ahead, you would have had all the time in the world to keep on working on your idea, make it even better and prepare it more perfectly. In the right moment you would have been ahead by the famous, profitable inch – or even more than that!

„*strengths or weaknesses,*

what is more important?"

<Franz X. Bühler>

Most people are of the misconception that they can only be successful when they have weeded out their weaknesses. Wrong!

How much energy do you need, if you want to strengthen one of your weaknesses even just a little bit? And when you have succeeded, worked hard and another weakness lies behind you, do you then feel fit and able to perform like a world champion in this area? Hardly…

Champions are made of strengths! The one who lives his strengths and develops them everyday does not have to be concerned about materialistic issues. Take for example Michael Schumacher. He loves driving a car, that is what he can do and that is what he does. Does he have to be concerned about his income?

There will always be some people whose strength is what you consider a weakness of yourself. Find them, delegate these tasks and do what you are strong at!

„Making decisions is one of the core characteristics of successful people"

<Franz X. Bühler>

If you want to or not: *»At one point you have to make a decision for everything, otherwise other people will do it for you.«* Is it that what you want? Imagine you are standing at a fork in the road and you are not quite sure which way is the right way. Then spread the facts on a table, consider carefully and make a decision! No matter what your decision will be, all directions lead to the goal. One might be a rough detour. On this way you have more valuable experiences which will most likely be of use to you at a later point, since experiences are the treasures of those who are successful! The one who does not make a decision remains at the fork and he is still standing there …(*smile) The world belongs to the deciders and not the hesitators! Resolution: *»The next time when I am in a restaurant I will make the decision what I want to eat within 30 seconds!«*

„if other people were

ambassadors and mirrors"

<Franz X. Bühler>

Ambassadors and mirrors, that is only esoteric drivel or is it not? Sure? The science of physics today clearly proves: *»Everything is a form of energy, a form of reverberation.«* Nothing can sound in you, if there is not the relevant „tuning fork".

Most esoterics however are of the opinion that the other person is your absolute mirror and therefore a clear ambassador of how you are, what your problems are. Wrong! Most „things" you discover about yourself thanks to others are often just a pure hint towards one of your drawers of thinking. They show that you have somewhere saved an experience which you today still connect with unpleasant feelings – and that this drawer is still active. That's it! This way to look at things becomes valuable if you can accept it with the following open attitude:

»If other people are the ambassador and mirror of myself, my inner „tuning forks", I will be thankful for everybody who „annoys me". He helps me to discover myself and to develop. Thank you!«

„old is the one, whose past

brings more joy

than the future"

<J. Knittel>

»You can't afford to have principles if you want to live to old age.« (Börne) *»How do you know that you are getting old? When you stop having hope and start remembering.«* (Sanders, collection) *»Nothing makes you become old faster than to always imagine, that one is getting older.«* (Lichtenberg, mixed writings). What do you think, is age a question of years or of your attitude. Is it a question of looks or inner fire? Do you also know people who are already old with 30, whose fire and passion faded, who feel and look like they see their everyday life – old and grey? The appropriate opinion of many people is: *»Your age is as you feel«*. Right! How old do you feel? No matter what your answer is. It is never too late! Make the decision now, to be young and vital in your mind and to stay like that, think about how you can realise that from today onwards – and your body will follow you!

„the good news:

you are always right“

<Franz X. Bühler>

You think: *»I have the nicest and best partner in the world?«* You are right! You think: *»It is difficult to start a flourishing business during a recession?«* You are right! You think: *»Even during a recession great ideas have good chances?«* You are right! You think: *»There is hardly money to make in your job. It is just hardly enough to live on.«* You are right! You think: *»Wow, I am in a very lucky situation. I have a good job, I make valuable experiences and still have the time to do some further training.«* You are right! You are always right! The world, your world is what you think of it. No matter what you think, you will be right! Doesn't that make you think? You are right: *»Think about that!«*

„Success is"

<Bessie A. Stanley>

»He has achieved success who has lived well,
laughed often and loved much;
who has enjoyed the trust of pure women, the respect
of intelligent men
and the love of little children;
who has filled his niche and accomplished his task;
who leaves the world better than he found it,
whether by an improved poppy,
a perfect poem, or a rescued soul;
who never lacked appreciation of earth's beauty
or failed to express it;
who looked for the best in others;
whose life was an inspiration and
whose memory a benediction.«

84

„catastrophes are chances"

<unknown>

September 11th 2001 was a catastrophe. But it was also a chance to help people who had trouble coping with a simple and effective NLP exercise. It was the chance to make air traffic even safer. It was the chance to check companies and diversify them so that they are now less liable to single risks. It was the chance for many people to give others support during a difficult time, to (finally) come closer to each other and be loved.

What kind of „catastrophe" are you in?

And what chances are hidden behind that? What do you make of it? What decisions do you make? Who are the persons with whom you can handle them?

„*everybody should be in favour of you and your ideas?*"

<Franz X. Bühler>

That is an unmistakable sign of a lacking self-assurance, a dented self-confidence and an even lower self-esteem!

Tough? Could be, but whatever you plan thoroughly, tackle full of determination and consequently carry through, there are always three types of reactions:

»*The ones who are against it and who will not use it, the ones who are still insecure and in the end will not decide in favour of it and the ones who are in favour of it, who really want it and support it.*«

You will never win everybody's support for your ideas! Forget it, it is solely your fault and you will be deterred from your great and inspiring ideas, because you are dying for recognition.

But you can also tackle it full of determination and goal-oriented because you are aware of your capability and the value of your idea and because you have the deep confidence that you will succeed and you are also aware that it will give some others – and especially you – a deep, inner satisfaction!

„the decisive factor is not

what you are, but

what you make of it"

<unknown>

Don't always run behind what you want to be, only because you are impressed by others. Analyse who you are and what you are good at, what are your absolute strengths – and make the best of it!

A physically challenged person in a wheelchair could moan and groan, he could feel sorry for himself and everybody would understand that. Does that help him? Does he feel happier because of that? Does he get the feeling that he is needed, precious and useful?

But he could also concentrate on his phenomenal staying power, his undestroyable self-motivation, his brilliant ability to think and become one of the most favourite and best motivational trainers. He knows what it means to make the best of what is available. People will buy that from him.

What is "paralysing" you? What are you super at and who could profit from that?

„don't start with a great resolution, but with little actions"

<saying>

»*The Road to Hell is paved with good resolutions*«, is what my teacher once told me when I tried to make him believe what my resolutions for the next year were. I was offended: »*Doesn't he believe in me?*«

Much later I understood what he meant. Indeed, we are making sooo many resolutions. Especially on New Year's eve – for the new year… But with the resolution itself almost nothing changes. It lulls us into a false sense of security that we already made a change, only because we realised something!

You know better. A resolution only then has a chance to become reality, when you do something small and you take that first step! What has been a resolution of yours for a long time that you haven't tackled yet?

V.

your thoughts,
your goldmine

„*about sowing and harvesting*"

<*basic law of the Universe*>

No farmer in his right mind would have the idea that he wants to harvest red, juicy strawberries, if he lovingly sowed corn in the spring.

He always harvests hard, yellow corn!

For every effect, no matter how special it is, a relevant cause preceded, for every reaction a relevant action preceded. That's pure physics.

You can't sow hate and harvest love. You can't think failure and rake in success. You can't sow mistrust and expect trust.

You accurately and precisely receive what you send, since you have trimmed your sending and receiving antenna for that!

Just think about it:

»*What do you want to sow today, in order to be able to harvest tomorrow? What causes do you want to set today in order to there effect tomorrow?*«

„*my subconsciousness –*

my garden"

<Franz X. Bühler>

Your subconciousness is like a wonderful, fruitful garden. Everything you plant will start to grow like a weed. And the plants to which you give the most attention and care will grow the strongest.

Do you want the problems which tear you to pieces, to grow? Do you want your overwhelming debts to grow? Or do you want your successes to grow rapidly, that the love in your relationship grows, flourishes and will be as beautiful, sparkling and exciting as never before?

Make a decision:

»*What do you want to have greater, stronger, more beautiful, powerful and exciting in your life?*« And then make an "action list" because only with „*knowing what you want*" little things change. You have to tackle it full of confidence, sow it in your „garden" and nourish it lovingly. When? Now, of course!

„*think – and it is*"

<Franz X. Bühler>

Whenever you think or supply your brain with some other kind of information, you literally burn in a response pattern into your computer. Visualising coins your responses as much as experiences, your education and your environment does, the culture goes along and the choice of your programmers like media, films, books and seminars. They all shape you in your whole comprehensive existence.

Before something can happen in your exciting life, it first has to be thought by you in some form. And the more intensive, clear and emotional you do that, the more effective your programming will be!

Example:*»Do you have a goal that drives and motivates you?«* Good, than imagine what it looks like when you have achieved this goal. See yourself in this absolutely fascinating movie. And then don't make the same mistake that most people make: *»They think, I have visualised it, now it has to happen.«* No! The next question is: *»What can I do today, in order to get one step closer towards that goal?«* Think first, then act!

93

„*emotions are the biggest source of power in our life*"

<Franz X. Bühler>

If you then are on your way full of confidence, you need wind, a lot of wind. Should there be none, you will need a motor and some fuel. Your emotions are your fuel, your wind! They are the accelerators of your wonderful journey. But be aware:

»*These sources of power work in all directions! No matter if love, joy, pleasure or hate, anger, envy and jealousy – some of them blow you forward, others slow you down or even drive you backwards!*«

Here is a well-tried idea as to how you can activate your mega power plant:»*Begrudge yourself 60 minutes of your precious time, look for pictures with great memories and write everything down that gives you pleasure, what motivates you, what you are proud of and then feel what happens…*« You can always read these power papers, when there is no wind that powerfully drives you. They are what causes your engine to start, so you go on with your goal-oriented journey!

„the most important person

in your life?"

<Franz X. Bühler>

Very simple. Look in the mirror and you know him.. Yes, you are the most important person in your wonderful and exciting life. And that is neither arrogant, nor egoistic!

Do you really like the picture in the mirror or are you one of the people who look in the mirror in the morning and say: »*Who is that in the mirror? – Yeah, yeah it's ok. I know that I like myself.*« Really? Are you sure? Just as you are, with all your characteristics? Good, then the following test should be very easy for you: »Just go ahead and shape – in front of the mirror – your mouth into a kiss. Look yourself into the eyes and gently and emotionally say: „I love you!"« (*smile)

Should you have weird feelings doing that, your mouth muscles do not really feel loose, you know that you still have some distance left on your way to self-love. How are others supposed to like you, if you are not able to do that yourself?

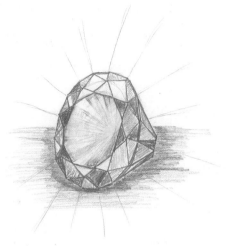

*Indem es gespalten wird und 56 mal
über die Schleifscheibe kratzt.
In dem es entdeckt und geschunden
wird findet es die Beachtung aller.
Ja sein Wert wird gar durch ein Monopol
geschützt.
Und doch wandelt es sich unter dem heftigsten
künstlichen Feuer zu Rauch, wie wir
Menschen auch.*

*By splitting it and by scratching it 56 times over the grinding
disc. By being discovered and maltreated it is taken note of by
everybody. Yes even its value is protected by a monopole.
And still it changes under the severe artificial fire into smoke,
just like we human beings do too.
The investment pays back. Through laborious precision work a
sparkling, precious treasure has been awakened!
Sometimes life seems to "grind" us, but he who believes in
„victory" will be richly rewarded.*

„*there is a winner*

also within you"

<Franz X. Bühler>

Question:
»*Would you take part in a race, together with 2 million other highly motivated participants if you knew today that only the winner will survive and everybody else would die?*«
»*I am not crazy!*« Do you think?
But you already did that! It was the race for the fertilisation of an egg. You were „the winner" and reached the cell first.
Congratulations! The winner syndrome stuck within you from the very start. But unfortunately it really seems to „stick" within many people instead of letting it flow. Let it go. It is supposed to unfold, grow and flourish. Create you own personal „winner album" and pay attention to the little wins and victories in everyday life. Write them down – and when you are not in a winning mood, read it. You will see, you will very quickly feel better.

„*the biggest chance of your life –*

your subconsciousness is blind!"

<Franz X. Bühler>

It automatically controls your body functions and lets everything grow that you put into it. You could compare it to a tape recorder which runs without interruption and constantly records everything that your sense canals supply.

But what is most important for your wishes, dreams and goals: »*Your subconciousness cannot distinguish between imagination, reality and dreams!*« Scary? Just the opposite! That is a chance of your lifetime! Just provide your memory regularly with clear pictures of your goals – in a way as if you had achieved them already. Then your subconciousness immediately starts to create circumstances that let you seize opportunities. Form your decisions so that the picture which was put in, as quickly as possible becomes your reality.

Do you want to bet…?

„Self-confidence, a subject for (almost) everybody"

<Franz X. Bühler>

Often arrogance is confused with strong self-confidence. The opposite is the case. Mostly an insecure, vulnerable character is hidden behind it. Lacking self-confidence is a subject for almost everybody – and that is not a shame! Even you were young at some point and that time your brain learned:*»I am young, the others are grown up, I am not able to do anything (yet), the others are able to do everything.«* Today you are grown up but your computer and the deeply anchored programmes are still exactly the same. Sure, some new things were added, but unfortunately the old, trained patterns still are as effective as they used to be. You want to change that? Then say to yourself several times loud and emotionally: *»I trust myself, I believe in my abilities.«* In order for the auto-suggestion to become effective even faster and more intensive, look for experiences in your life which exactly prove these words. Make up a list and regularly read it. After a little while this new picture of yourself will be anchored – a person full of confidence in itself!

„*my subconsciousness,*

my tape, my CD, my

DVD, my PC"

<Franz X. Bühler>

If you have recorded the music of Louis Armstrong on a tape, does it play Michael Jackson melodies?
No: »*It plays Louis Armstrong!*« What do you expect when you record a blue movie on a DVD? A math programme for children? No: »*It will play a blue movie!*« And what do you expect when you save a text programme on your computer? Will it show as an accounting programme? Surely, it will play the text programme…
And what is the result, when your brain, your sub-conciousness, saves action, crime thrillers, murder and manslaughter, horror news, negative headlines, dramas and sitcoms?
A well-balanced, loving, harmonious, motivated, goal-oriented person? Make a decision what you want to have and then choose wisely!

„if you could choose,

what kind of a person you are"

<Franz X. Bühler>

How would you decide? Would you be a loving partner? Quiet, well-balanced and in harmony? Full of self-confidence and self-acceptance? Diligent, disciplined and with a strong staying power? Willing and eager to learn? Sporty, healthy and fit? Easy to get along with and tolerant? Hard, but fair, with a clear line? Far-sighted, courageous, motivated and with a great memory? Reads and knows a lot? Loves and accepts people how they are? Concentrated and creative? Loving and tidy? Can show happiness? Can let go? Is honest? That is good: *»You can choose!«*
Choose now how you want to be and then lovingly and carefully write it down with the following words:
»I am ....«
Two times a day joyfully read this exciting text and imagine what it is like when you are already this interesting, popular person!

VI.

wealth – more than a word, within word, within reach and feasible

„*is materialistic wealth*

also your wish?"

<is a core question for many people>

Once somebody said: *»money is only a subject, when you don't have enough of it.«* This painful experience I can only acknowledge. However, this saying only helped me partly.

First you have to clean up the mixed emotions, which always come up when money is a subject. Wanting to have money has nothing to do with filthy lucre. You surely live in a culture where it is important. Money is nothing more or less than a neutral measure of exchange. It is a yardstick of your effect and not of intelligence and hard work. Money is great and beautiful – and if you want to help somebody, then think about it, you can only give something that you have, no matter if it is money, love or acknowledgement.

Bodo Schaefer has an effective tip for that: *»Ask yourself what are your „income-producing-activities" (IPA's) How can you be useful to others?«* And then every day take care of these IPA's!

„*the simplest principle*

for wealth"

<basic formula>

It is that simple it almost seems ridiculous. Don't underestimate it! There is more to it than you first might think. The formula reads as follows:

»Every day spend less than you earn!«

Not the large earnings make you rich, your intelligent use of the dear money can make you rich or poor. Sure, if you have debts, you have to pay them off first, you are in a quandary. Then there is only one thing that helps: *»analyse how much you definitely and regularly earn, then plan your expenses and amortizations and keep strictly to it.«* And one more thing is very important: *»Plan so that you can put 10% of your income aside – even during the amortisation of your debts!«*

If you think this way takes too long, look around, to whom and in what form your abilities and experiences can be of use, what other additional valuable activities are at your disposal and by doing so generate more income.

„he who doesn't respect the penny

doesn't deserve the pound"

<piece of popular wisdom>

Did you ever ask yourself what the much sought-after million is made of? Correct, from many individual Pounds, Francs, Euros etc.

We do the most impossible things in order to get the passionately longed-for million into our life. We play lotto, roulette, take part in competitions and much more.

»If I had one million, everything would be very different. I would welcome it like a dear friend, pamper it and take good care of it.«

That is absurd, an absolute joke! And what is it with the individual money unit – the Pound, the Franc and the Euro? They are the brothers and sisters, which make up one million! We treat them like dirt, disparaging and carelessly spend them, according to the principle: *»That doesn't cost a lot, what are 20 Pounds, Euros or Francs?«* Do you really want to become wealthy? Then check yourself and observe: *»How do you treat change?«*

„saving is fun,

when I measure it"

<Franz X. Bühler>

The most boring part of saving is that you cannot grant yourself a treat from that. The little (unnecessary) treats. Sure, I can buy something later. I hope so! Has the time come and I buy myself something, it is not saving anymore. It is the pure opposite. I spend money! So my brain has to learn having fun when saving and not only when spending money!
The following attitude can help you with that: *»Saving is not renunciation, it means achieving a goal on a different level.«* And this is how it works:

1. Set yourself a saving goal, which you think you can easily achieve.
2. Double your goal, you can do more than you think.
3. Draw a measuring unit with your saving goal at the top.
4. Every day write down what you have achieved so far.
5. Lay down to which rewards you treat yourself when you have achieved 10,20,30% etc.

Even the most precious diamonds only then sparkle with their fullest splendour if also „the diamonds" sparkle in the inside of a human being.

„in order to become wealthy,

discover the wealth in your life"

<Franz X. Bühler>

Do you really want to draw wealth into your life? Really? And what is it worth to you? What are you prepared to do for it? Still „YES"? Ok, then let's go for it! The indispensable basis for that is that you build up a burning, magically magnetic emotion for wealth within you and that every day you put some more „coal" on it just like you do with a fireplace!

The following exercise will help you with that – and is still free: *»From today on, concentrate every day, wherever you are, on the wealth around you. Pay attention to the well-built roads, the signs, the traffic lights, the houses, the cars, the jewellery, the clothes, the warm room, the television, the radio, the trees which carry fruit, the beautiful flowers, the food which is always available, your health, your abilities.«* Pay attention to that and you will discover: *»The world is full of wealth!«*

In order to become and stay wealthy you first have to feel wealthy deep within yourself.

Yes, flare up the deep feeling of wealth within you!

109

„I am a

value generator!"

<unknown>

If you manufacture a complicated work piece for your boss and he gets more money for it, than he spent on material and work, you have created something of value. If you sell the customer a great product, with which he feels happy and wealthier, than if his money was still in the bank , you are a generator of values. If you help somebody, offer him good advice and he has greater benefit from that, than what he has paid you, you are a generator of values. If you paint a wonderful picture and the buyer has more joy in it, than if he had saved his money, you are a generator of values. Become aware: *»With what are you generating values? What is it that makes your work so valuable to others?«*

And then be happy and say 100 times loud and clear: *»I am a generator of values!«*

110

VII.

Wisdoms of great thinkers – understand and convert into action

„*you are what you think,*

all day long"

<Henry David Thoreau>

»*What are the attitudes and emotions you would like to live with tomorrow?What is your future supposed to look like?*« In order to tomorrow lead the exciting and fulfilling life, that you sincerely wish for yourself, in order to be the popular and idolised person you want to be, you have to think it first today! Therefore make a decision now:

»*How and what would you like to be? What attitudes and emotions help you with that?*« And then ask yourself: »*Where in your life did you already have these attitudes and emotions? Who are the people you know who are like you want to be? How does your day tomorrow look when it proceeds according to your wishes?*«

And now another hot tip:

»*The things you think about before falling asleep, have an ongoing effect during the night. They anchor and grow stronger!*« Make use of this valuable insight!

„the story of an orange"

After a student tried without success to sell oranges on behalf of his master at a market, he returned completely demotivated and angrily raved against the people who did not want to buy his oranges. The master shook his head and asked the student: *»If I squeeze this orange what comes out of it?« »Orange juice of course«* the student replied. *»Right – and when I hit it with a hammer, what will then come out of it?« » Also orange juice«* the student grumbled. *»...and if a mule steps on it, what will then come out of it?« »It will always be orange juice«* the student replied obviously agitated. His master then said with a calm voice: *»the orange will always reply with what is inside it, no matter what happens to it. Put a person under pressure. Does he react with hate, anger and envy then that is what is inside him.«* What comes out of you when you are under pressure? In order for love to come out, you first have to learn to love and accept yourself. A sentence that could help you with that is the suggestion: *»I love and accept myself.«* Say it loud and clearly to yourself for six months every day 50 times a day and be happy!

„faith moves mountains"

<1.Corinthian 13,2.>

Already Friedrich Schiller said:
»To him nothing on earth remains unwrenched and firm who has no faith.«
I don't mean faith in the religious sense of the word. Faith also means to be deeply and intensively convinced of something, without the slightest doubt! Doubts are the quietly nagging destroyers of great ideas! Therefore do everything that can strengthen your faith in the success of your project.
And here another tip: *»Before you talk to somebody about your great goal, strengthen and anchor it within yourself!«*
Every wish, every dream, every goal is at its beginning a small plant. In this moment, doubts, objections and "well-meant" advice can easily destroy it. Before you start to spread to others, ask yourself the following question: *»What do you have to believe so that it is possible to achieve your goal? What else can contribute to that? When and where did you already have these abilities, this knowledge, these resources at your disposal?«*

„freedom is the possibility

to realise own goals"

<unknown>

Don't we live in great times? The whole world is at our feet. You can travel anywhere you like; do the job that you like, realise ideas that are important to you. What do you need for that? Knowledge and skills!
Knowledge is the basic prerequisite in order to do something. But it only turns into a "skill" by courageous actions. That is great! Almost all of the world's knowledge lies openly in front of you. Go to the next library and during your entire life you will not be able to read what is written there. Surf the Internet and your world of knowledge grows exponentially! You have the freedom to start right here, to tackle your goals full of determination and to realise them. Who but yourself can prevent you from doing that? Do it now!

„the secret of being able to

lies in wanting to"

<unknown>

To come along "being able to do something" is rarely an art. Your common sense and basic talents for your desired „being able to" go further than you think. The rest you can accomplish by exercising, exercising and again exercising.

But what is the key to consequent exercising, when it is so funny? What is needed to digest painful failures and to stand up again every time when you are slammed back onto the floor of „reality". Nothing else but your will. We all know that.

The question is: *»What can you do when there seems to be a little man inside yourself who just then wants to convince you that it doesn't make any sense and that it would be better to give up?«*

Then again visualise what becomes possible when you hold out. How your life will be when you will have achieved your goal. Couldn't it be that right now you are just one tiny step away from your desired success. You would never forgive yourself if you gave up.

„*individually we are words,*

together a poem"

<unknown>

A symphony consists of thousands of notes. Individually they are just simply tones, together they form a complete, beautiful and harmonious composition. By yourself you are a melodious, important tone in the universe. Without you something would be missing in this piece of music!

But you can only completely develop when you see yourself as a part of the whole. How?

Your contribution to this miracle lies hidden in your abilities and talents. Discover them, start to polish and cut these wonderful diamonds and make them sparkle! And the best part of it is: »*You will see that when you awaken everything and you do what is hidden deeply as a masterpiece within you since you were born, all your problems will dissolve by themselves.*«

119

„when you eat, then eat,

when you walk, then walk,

when you run, then run"

<Zen-wisdom>

But that is what I already do. Are you sure? Are you really sure? Isn't it more like that: *»When you eat, you think of walking – and when you're walking, you already think of running? Do what your are doing right now consciously and with full concentration – and only that!«* What is your gain from that? Concentration fosters more rapid, precise results, the quality of your work increases and your additional gains are inner silence, you live healthier and you have more time! And time is especially important today. It pays to make better use of it this way. You think that when you do several things simultaneously you will proceed quicker? This is very wrong! Make the following test: *»Remove everything from your desk that you don't need right now and only put on it what you are working on at this time.«* You will find out how much more efficient and quicker you will be!

„I have never been poor, only broke,

being poor is a frame of mind"

<Mike Todd>

»*Being broke is a temporary situation…*« To change a deeply anchored inner picture is harder than getting up after having fallen and trying to tackle it once again! Do you know the saying: »*The rich always get richer and the poor always get poorer.*« Why? Because both, wealth and poverty are a question of inner attitude and not external circumstances. The rich man has to „defend" his wealth everyday just as the poor man does his poverty!

But the desired change can only come from the inside. How? Every day observe: »*How have you behaved in monetary situations today, what decisions did you make?*« Analyse thoroughly and honestly – and change this movie in your thoughts in a way as if you already did it right. With astonishment you will discover that you will act differently the next time you are in the same situation and that your „old" pattern of reaction will become obvious to you while you are acting.

„today is my best day"

<book by Arthur Lassen>

A clever person once said: *»Every morning when I get up, I have the choice to be happy and to be pleased or to be unhappy and feel miserable. I am not stupid, I choose being happy!«*
Maybe you think: *»It's not that simple. It's easy for him to say that. If he had my concerns, he also would not be happy.«*
Question: *»Under what circumstances can you better handle concerns and problems? When you are full of power and happy or when you disheartenedly think about solutions?«* Surely when you are full of power and joie de vivre! That doesn't make your problem smaller (not yet) but changes your attitude in dealing with it. That is the only way to alter course and find the right way.
How? Draw up a list with things, experiences that build you up and motivate you. Read it once daily and once again experience in your thoughts those beautiful, power-stimulating moments or read „my ipowerbook" by the author Franz X. Bühler.

„*take your time*"

<unknown>

Take your time to work,
it is the price of success.
Take your time to think,
it is the source of power.
Take your time to play,
it is the secret of youth.
Take your time to read,
it is the fundamental of knowledge.
Take your time to be friendly,
it is the gate to being happy.
Take your time to dream,
it leads the way to the stars.
Take your time to love,
it is the real joie de vivre.
Take your time to be merry,
it is the music of the soul.
Take your time!

„living means learning

from nature"

<unknown>

Learning from the sun – to warm.
Learning from the clouds – to float.
Learning from the wind – give impulses.
Learning from the birds – gain elevation.
Learning from the trees – standing firm.

Learning from the flowers – learning to shine.
Learning from the stones – learning to persevere.
Learning from the leaves in autumn – learning to let go.

Learning from rules – to exude oneself.
Learning from the earth – to change.
Learning from the moon – to change.
Learning from the stars – that life always goes on,
always starts anew.

„there are no outsiders

in this world"

<Dr. Joseph Murphy

Do you feel useless, is the whole world crashing down around you and you think, "nothing makes sense", then think about it:
»There are no outsiders in our world, every human being has his place.
You too are needed!
Find out, to whom and how your abilities are useful and then make your decisions!«
It is your special abilities, which are in demand – and not your weaknesses!
Now ask yourself immediately – and write it down:
»What are you especially good at? What are your strengths? What makes you so precious?«
Every human being is a part of the whole, no matter how strange or odd he seems to be to you. He is needed! And if only for the reason that you and others can further develop!

VIII.

Habits that will be of help to you

„just do it"

<Nike>

Start to tackle your most important, most unpleasant and most depressing subject today. One that has cost you a lot of energy in the past, which often prevented you, yes even paralysed you, and which you kept putting off much too long with an uncomfortable feeling.

Think it through and divide it into small, makeable jobs. And then you tackle it full of determination and reward yourself after achieving every interim goal!

Curiously look back at the end of the day and enjoy the pleasantly warm tingling in your stomach, the proud, satisfying feeling to be a person of deed. You have turned from a neglector into a doer! Congratulations!

The recipe is: *»Do it!«*

„what can I do today

to get a step closer towards

my goals?“

<The key question of successful people>

And even if it is just a small step besides the many important and absolutely necessary actions, take it. Every day take another step full of confidence in the direction of your motivating and energy-loaded wishes, dreams and goals.

Determine this unique step first thing in the morning or even better, the evening before and take this first step reliably and consequently!

When you every day, deep within yourself, feel how you get closer to your wonderful goals, incredible and undreamt-off power will be created.

You will see, already after a short time, an exciting, expectations full and invincible power will grow inside you and you can't wait to plan the next step to success and taking it!

The patience of this bamboo farmer has paid off. Tall, powerful and beautiful it stands. The reward for four years of loving care.

„patience, a virtue

which is often forgotten..."

<shortened example, Bamboo, from the book
"Gesetze der Gewinner" by Bodo Schäfer>

»To plant bamboo requires long-term thinking and confidence. First the bamboo farmer plants the sprouts into the ground. Then he covers the earth's surface with hay. Every morning the farmer waters the still invisible sprouts. He removes weed and loosens the soil. Every morning – four long years, in which he doesn't see his sprouts, in which he doesn't know if his efforts will be rewarded and he also doesn't know if they are still alive. Finally, at the end of the fourth year, the sprouts break through the surface. And then they will grow a whole 20 metres in only 90 days!«

What are you waiting for? What have you sowed, without exactly knowing when and if it shoots?
Continue, hang in, take care of and pamper your seeds and look forward to the day, when they first show their delicate tips in order to then „shoot up from the ground" with invincible power!

„time is my

most precious source"

<Hans Peter Zimmermann>

The only thing we can really „loose" in our life is time. Once gone, it is lost for always and forever! Time is life. Time is our way to measure existence! Replace the expression „time" with the word „life" and then judge yourself: *»I don't have time. Waste time.«* They will turn into: *»I have no life. Waste life«*.

Pareto's 80/20 rule brings it to the point: *»Almost always we achieve 80% of the results with 20% effort. In 20% of the time we accomplish 80% of productive work. With 20% of customers we achieve 80% of the sales. In 20% of the time we make 80% of our experiences.«* Now imagine what would be possible if you used 50% of your time properly!

I have noticed that always when I said the following sentence loud to myself 50 times in the morning and 50 times in the evening, I started to automatically make better use of my time.

»Time is my most precious source, therefore I make good use of it for activities which lead to results.«

„speech is silvern"

<part of popular wisdom>

and silence is golden, says a popular saying. That might be true in many cases but in an equal number of cases it is completely wrong. And it contradicts all quantum physical knowledge! The couple who sits in front of the television passively every day, hurries from visit to visit during the weekend, constantly makes boring invitations, individually takes care of their social life in a club, avail themselves of all meetings in committees which brings them an ego-boost etc. should not be surprised, when suddenly there is nothing to talk about. Therefore: *»Take your destiny into your hands full of determination or rather into your mouth and talk! Talk about this, that and everything, exchange exciting experiences no matter what, but talk.«* The power of communication is one of the most precious presents which we received when we were born. Only silence lets people grow apart!

133

„*never – never – never give up*"

<Churchill's shortest speech>

In the moment you give up, when you stop looking further and stop believing in a solution, the whole thing collapses with a loud bang. Many would understand you – yes they would even encourage you to finally accept that something doesn't work! You have cramped up, given everything, sacrificed yourself to the point of exhaustion. You proved how important it is to you. Now you should be allowed to give up with a clear conscience. Shouldn't you?

No – Don't do it! When you now give up, you are destroying a part of your self-confidence and self-esteem. No matter what it has cost you so far, those were investments in your education! Do you want them to have been in vain?

Not to give up doesn't mean that you force something. It can mean: »*If one way didn't lead you to the goal, then it is another way. There is one – find it!*«

Inform yourself, who already successfully managed the problem, this challenge – and then ask this person for advice!

„*discover the beauty*

in others"

<Franz X. Bühler>

Today shall become a unique and special day. Together we will go on a voyage of discovery of a very special kind! *»Look for something nice in every person you meet!«*
That could be a simple detail like a well-shaped nose, beautifully curved lips, the pleasant voice, precious jewellery or the well-kept clothing which he/she is wearing, his tolerant ways towards you or others.
It doesn't matter what it is….And now observe yourself: *»How do you feel when you do this?«* And how do the people affected react to that? Yes, they too will act differently, as you, with the choice of different thoughts, change your aura. The way you approach people, comes back to you sooner or later!
What do you think of the idea, to constantly get used to this „discoverer syndrome" – and by doing that turn into a pleasant person who is always welcome? What do you think, how much easier will things be for you if you act this way?

„do what you are afraid of

and the end of being afraid

will be certain"

How many times have you put off unpleasant things, which you reluctantly approached, and which command a lot of respect or which almost paralysed you because you were afraid of them? You found a thousand reasons why today it can't be done.

That is completely nonsensical and paradoxical:

»To carry things which you put off around with you all the time, is the same as if you did a mountain hike, collected stones and hiked another mountain with a backpack that is still filled with the stones from the day before. It gets heavier day by day. It puts a strain on you and deprives you unnecessarily of your precious power.«

Be honest: *»Almost always the thing that you had put off a long time, was taken care of in no time and it was mostly only half as bad as you had thought!«*

Do the important things today, as tomorrow they will become urgent – and after you have done so pay attention to your emotions!

„the 72-hour rule"

<unknown>

Everything that you have planned to do and did not accomplish or at least taken the first steps toward within 72 hours, unfortunately holds a great probability that you will never do it! And it first even weakens your self-confidence.

Whenever you are enthusiastic about something, whether about something that is in this book, an exciting seminar, a good tip, that somebody gives you, immediately do the following: *»Consciously plan this activity, this behaviour, write it on the agenda and – do it, take the first step within 72 hours!«*

You will see, it will make you really proud to be a person of deed instead of words. Only the things you do will have an effect – it is not what you don't do or about what you only talk. In your funeral address nobody will mention what you had planned and then didn't do. You will be measured by your actions. What is it that you absolutely want to do within the next 72 hours? Do it!

„are you already

keeping a success diary?“

<Bodo Schaefer>

What that is?

A success diary is a book, folder or notebook, in which you enter all your large, middle and small successes. Everything that you are proud of, that created a good feeling inside yourself. Things that are handled consequently and are taken care off. etc.

Successes like: *»Full of discipline I made 3 telephone calls, which I had put off for a long time. I offered another person a kind word, paid him a compliment. I helped an old person across the street. Today I finally remembered to water the flowers.«*

What that's good for?

If you do that consequently, it is the absolutely most favourable idea to strengthen your self-confidence and self-esteem. And this is something that has suffered at some point with 99% of all people.

And the one who thinks that this doesn't apply to him, might be in need of that the most!

„great things

flourish in silence"

<unknown>

Are you able to work fully concentrated when you are amidst a big party? Do you really believe that the birth of great ideas is possible, when around you things are exploding? Based on the scientific knowledge of the brain today, this is hardly possible.

Allow yourself your well-deserved peace and quiet, leave the hectic daily routine behind you and systematically close your still open active „windows"! Only then will you be able to load your „RAM", your main memory with things, that you need for the wonderful birth of new ideas, creations or project solutions.

And now ask your super computer specific questions and give it enough time to go through possible creative combinations. Great ideas often make themselves felt with a tender, fine voice. How do you want to hear it, when „noise" drowns everything all around?

„do as if“

<unknown>

The famous clown Rolf Knie was once asked in an interview: *»What happens when a clown receives a depressing message just before his appearance? How can he be funny in such a moment and still delight people and carry them away?«*

His short answer: *»Do as if! Do as if you were in a good mood, as if nothing happened, give everything you have and get completely wrapped up in your role, live it with all your senses. You will see, already after a short while you will start to feel exactly like that!«*

Do as if you already were this enthusiastic, precious person who you want to be. Get interested in the vacations and houses, which you will allow yourself to take and have. Visit exhibitions, where you will find everything that will belong in your exciting life. Surround yourself with people who are already where you would like to be.

But beware: *»Don't mix „do-as-if“ with already booking the vacations, ordering your dream car, buying clothes in expensive boutiques, which today you can't afford!«*

First in your head, then step by step on the „outside“!

140

„only when you know what you are searching for, will you be able to find it"

The story of the jinxed corkscrew…
You are standing in your kitchen in front of an open drawer which is filled with a vast amount of chrome-shining cutlery, ladles, knives and other "household tools" and you are convulsively looking for a corkscrew. *»I can't find it«*…you shout towards your partner. *»But it has to be there. Look one more time«*. You desperately keep on looking. It is jinxed. You just can't get a hold of this jin…corkscrew.
»What does it look like?« you grumble, impatiently and irritated. *»It has an orange handle«*. The moment you heard „orange" it catches your eye. It was there all the time, directly in front of your eyes. You didn't notice it, because you didn't know what to look for. It is the same with all things in our life: *»Only if you know what you are searching for, will you be able to find it!«* What are you searching for? What answers? What should your life be like? Different? Different in what respect? Ask your brain exact questions and you will get exact answers!

„the story of an onion"

<Franz X. Bühler>

You definitely feel it. Somewhere deep inside you know there must be a huge knot, something that stands in your way again and again? You work at yourself, develop and seem to go around in circles, you don't seem to get any further?

Then the following analogy might help you: *»Every human being is a complex creature with an infinite number of experiences and other learning processes. It is like an onion!«* If you want to proceed to the core, it can be good to first remove some skin. Unfortunately you will never know how far you have already proceeded, as the desired goal has not been achieved, yet.

There is only one help:

»Keep on doing it consequently!«

You are worth it! Who knows, may be you are just one „skin" away from you long-wished for solution! Never, never, never give up. Otherwise you will never experience what it would be like, if...

Oh, and by the way, it is normal that onions cause tears when you peel their skin.

142

IX.

Things that make life easier

„*you're feeling weak?*

Change your attitude"

<from neurolinguistical programming (NLP)>

There are moments in which we feel weak and drained, that is normal. It is not normal to remain in this state. You could of course wait and hope that somebody comes by and says something fantastic to you which will lift you up again. Or you could start to handle it with determination yourself.

What do you want?

If you want to do it yourself, the following exercise will be of help to you:

»Sit or stand upright, chest out, shoulders lifted, smile, show your teeth, take a deep breath, close your eyes and when exhaling think of a special moment in your life, then knock seven times on your breastbone.« Repeat the whole thing ten times. Then bend your arms, as if you wanted to show somebody your strong upper arm muscles, take another deep breath and when exhaling say out loud and clear: *»yeees – yeah-I am great!«* And now sense how you feel!

„who'll receive the gift

of a kind word today?"

<differently today>

We as human beings are remarkably special. Criticism "well-meant as always?" – and other „kind tips and hints" we give or offer much too quickly.

When was the last time that you consciously looked for the exciting, unique and positive in another person? Make the following, fascinating test today:

»In reference to the people in your surroundings, at home and at work, pay attention to the things that especially catch your eye and which you can honestly praise. Make a gift with a generous compliment and whisper somebody a kind word in their ear. Write "I love you" with a bright red lipstick on the bathroom mirror to your partner and watch closely what happens. Observe attentively, listen to yourself, feel what your emotions are and decide, when you grant yourself such an exciting day the next time.« You honestly deserve it!

„do good

and talk about it"

<unknown>

Pay attention to the order, as it is the deciding factor: *»Do it first, then talk about it!«* And not, as many people tend to do it, talk about it first – and then they often never do it. The one who talks about it first is still looking for acknowledgement. He is not sure about what he wants to do.

Warning: *»That is the most dangerous moment in the life of an idea!«*

If now somebody comes and doubts it, he often succeeds to nip even the greatest ideas in their bud. He nourishes nagging doubts in you!

It is very different and much more effective if you talk about it after you have accomplished your work! It means to give something energy, to increase and to spread it, to stir enthusiasm , yes even a little envy in others – and not to be selfishly the centre of attention. The only question is, when and how you talk about it! By the way: *»Envy has to be gained!«*

„Conflicts, rage, anger and hatred,

how others take away your energy"

<The Celestine Insights – the third>

When you argue, get annoyed, get furious or angry, your precious energy flows directly to the person who is affected by your dispute, your anger, your fury.

The next time observe curiously how you feel after such an incident which was so full of energy. Are you feeling strong, balanced and full of tremendous energy? Hardly.

When you get into such a situation again, test one of the following effective ideas. Give the other person a loving hug and say to him: *»If you need energy you can get it from me.«* Should this not be possible, take a deep breath and say or think: *»I was annoyed and angry but despite this fact I find this/that about her/ him beautiful and lovely.«* Difficult? May be – but with astonishing effects!

„he who is afraid

has already lost"

<unknown>

Fear can be one of the meanest and power-sapping emotions that we know. But it can also protect or even drive you. Of which nature is your fear? Does it help you to courageously move along full of motivation – or does it paralyse you? Answer the following questions:

- Do you have fears or doubts in any form about a possible result?
- Are there other apprehensions or doubts?
- What does your life look like if what you're afraid of, does definitely not happen?
- What would be the worst that could happen, when your apprehensions definitely come true?
- Is that really so bad?
- What can you do right now, to get rid of these apprehensions and fear?

»Being afraid of – means concentrating on the wrong thing! You are directing your energy towards something that you do not want to have!«

„he who bears a grudge,

has his own trials

and tribulations"

<Franz X. Bühler>

We as human beings are special creatures. How many times do we get annoyed with somebody and carry this grudge even for years? And who has all the work due to this „grudge carrying" – the other person or you? No animal would do that. The good news:
»There is a solution – it is called „forgiving"!«
Although tremendously effective, it seems to be one of the most difficult things we know. And additionally to forgive would be extremely healthy! Not to forgive often leads to inner cramps, ulcers or even cancer! Do you want that? I know it is easier said than done, and when it really counts it can be damn difficult. Therefore try the following: *»Imagine in your inner thoughts that your kind child goes to the inner child of another person, shakes his hand and asks for forgiveness in regards to xyz.«* Will it work? Try it!

150

„everything is difficult,

before it gets easy"

<unknown>

How many times have people said to you: *»Wow, what you are doing there is difficult. I could never do that!«* And you replied: *»Oh no, it's very easy.«* Why? Because you are able to do it, because you are in command of it, it seems to be easy for you.

That's how everything works. In the beginning they seem difficult, because we don't have the hang of it. The more we practise, the easier it gets, yes, we could even tackle other challenges.

No matter what your plans are: *»It may, yes it should seem difficult to you in the beginning.«* If it does it not do that, then the goal, the wish, the dream, the challenge is too small. You can only grow from things which challenge you.

They will take you further!

Everything is a part of it. The hard and strenuous sweat-producing work in the vineyard, the picking of the sun-ripened grapes, the care-taking of the precious juice of the vine – and enjoying the fine full-bodied drops after a hard day's work has been completed.

„you deserve it to enjoy the balance between work and pleasure with a clear conscience"

<Franz X. Bühler>

Aren't we crazy? We work and slog away day and night and don't grant ourselves any breaks. Often our family and friends even eating fall by the wayside. And if we allow ourselves even once the luxury to come to work at noon, we have a guilty conscience. That can't be!

We know that we have deserved the breaks, but deep inside this obtrusive, low voice successfully whispers this unpleasant feeling again and again.

Did you also discover that within yourself, or do you know somebody like that? Then it is time for the suggestion *„I deserve to enjoy the balance between work and pleasure with a clear conscience"*. Write it on a card and say it out loud 50 times in the morning and 50 times in the evening. Do this for 4 weeks and you will be amazed!

153

„*do you already have*

a dream album?"

<*Bodo Schaefer*>

No? Then it is high time! Now today open your personal dream album. Collect pictures of all the things you would like to have. Write in it what is important to you, what you want to "draw" into your wonderful and exciting life. Colour it in your thoughts, in your daydreams, lively and powerfully. Make a collage from these pictures and briefly look at it every day:
»*It will become your life.*«
Automatically? No, but by this you anchor a response basis for it – and that is one of the key conditions that this full and active life, this lifetime dream can become your reality.
The fool only looks at the pictures and thinks: »*Too bad, it will hardly ever come true.*« The clever one asks himself: »*How can I get there?*« The clever one already has a plan and the most clever asks: »*What can I do today, to…?*«

„when a monkey peers in, you can't expect an apostle to look out"

<Lichtenberg – about physiognomics>

When a looser looks in, no winner can look out. When an ugly person looks in, no beautiful person can look out. When a worker looks in, no CEO can look out. When an angry person looks in, no happy person can look out. When a poor person looks in, no millionaire can look out. You see, it is the same everywhere.

It is always looking at you, what you expect, what you think of yourself, how you feel!

Change your thoughts, change your opinion about yourself, change your attitude and the person who you want to be, looks at you. Do it until you feel it deep in your heart, what you want to see, and the step to get there is shorter and easier than you can believe today.

Yes, you are totally ok. You are great. You are precious!

„*did somebody annoy you?*"

Human beings are very special creatures. Again and again we allow ourselves to get annoyed. That doesn't mean anything else than: >*We are choosing annoying emotions!*< But the paradox in this can already be seen in our own words! We tend to say: »*I got annoyed!*«

I – myself – got annoyed! Such a joke! Nobody in the world can get you annoyed, if you don't allow it. You have to do it to yourself. Despite this, we give other people the power over our emotions again and again. Be honest: »*How do you feel when you get annoyed?*« Full of energy, powerful, motivated or without energy, powerless, more demotivated?

The best that you can do right now is to plan: »*Today I will not get annoyed.*« Or positively said: »*Today I will remain quiet and calm. I myself control my feelings, no matter who or what approaches me!*«

And if you should get annoyed again, get used to tag on a positive additional remark. For example: »*Oh boy, is this an a..., but he drives a nice car, I have to admit that.*« What this is good for? With this additional remark your brain in retrospect links the annoyance with something pleasant and you immediately feel better. Truth is what works!

„letting go?" ·

<Franz X. Bühler>

Letting go can mean:
- Accept the IS-state! It is as it is. You cannot change the past. But the way you think about it today, strongly influences your future.
- Don't judge! Judging means „not accepting", holding on to it, to give it energy.
- Don't concentrate in a specific way! That means limitation. A specific goal? Yes. But the way shall remain flexible.
- Don't doubt that you will achieve your goal. Therefore set yourself goals, in which you can believe!
- Pass on everything from your life, what you don't need any longer, e.g. what you haven't used in a year. This means creating space for new things, for what you expected.
- You don't need „wanting-to-be-right" to prove that others are "not-right".
- Be free of „having-to-win!" The more, for example, you can let go while playing a game, the better are paradoxically your chances of winning.

„learning faster?

through modelling"

<Franz X. Bühler>

When did you make the biggest and fastest learning progress in your life? Right, when your were still a baby and later a child, soaking up like a dry sponge and full of curiosity explored the word full of thirst for knowledge.

You learned how to eat, walk, run, make a phone call and how to react accordingly in specific situations.

And how did you learn that? You watched your parents, studied your environment and simply copied everything until you were just as successful. In NLP we call this: *»You have modelled!«*

This still works as it did when you were a child. You want to be successful in tennis, golf, track and field, in football, in your job? Then look for models, people who already are good at what you want to learn, and model them. Copy them. Act the same way. Get into the habit of doing the same things and you will celebrate the same success. What and how would you like to be?

„*you need*

more energy – instantly?"

<Franz X. Bühler>

Then drink 2 to 3 litres of water a day. We human beings consist of 70% water. Then it is only logical, what our body is thirsty for in the true sense of the meaning.

Enough water means: *»Better digestion, thinner blood, your nerve tracts conduct better, you'll get a clearer head and you will feel more vital and more fit.«* The side effect can be, that you get even rid of your gnawing headache (that is if you have any) from which you suffered a long time, as these often are a cause of too little fresh clear water.

And now to the oxygen:

The next time you feel weak and powerless make the following test: *»Take deep breathes while you slowly count to 6, hold your breath and count to 24, then slowly exhale and count to 12.«* This you do 3 times. A slight dizziness will be caused for a short period of time. But after that, I guarantee you, you will feel much more fit. If it helps? *»The proof of the pudding is in the eating!«*

„*furious or angry?*"

<unknown>

Then test the following magic formula. In your thoughts imagine this person or this situation and say to yourself: »*May peace be with you!*«
You will see, you will instantly feel much better and a quiet, pleasant emotion will make itself felt!
That might sound funny, yes almost mysterious, but it isn't. In NLP this form of anchoring is called „chaining-anchor".
In this moment the brain links the picture that creates fury and anger with this very special sentence, which we already connect with peaceful, pleasantly quiet emotions. The effect is so emphatic because this short sentence has been used and formed already a billion times – and it is said every week again and again! In regards to quantum physics you so to speak hitch up to a well-tried and deeply anchored response pattern. Does this really work? Only your own test can prove it. »*May peace be with you!*«